Hockey Mom, Hockey Dad

"Brilliantly comic and touching.... A show as energized with the shock of recognition as winter and the Stanley Cup.... It's amazing."

— Stephen Pedersen,
The Chronicle Herald

"Always funny and insightful...*Hockey Mom, Hockey Dad*...proves that Melski has a keen understanding of the people of his generation...."

— Ken Chisholm,
What's Goin' On

"An artist to watch!"

— *NOW* magazine

"One of our hottest young playwrights."

— *The Daily News*

HOCKEY MOM, HOCKEY DAD

A PLAY IN TWO ACTS

Michael Melski

Breton Books

Editor: Ronald Caplan

Production Assistance: Bonnie Thompson

Front Cover Photo: "Miners' Forum, Glace Bay, undated. High School Hockey Team" by Leslie Shedden. Our thanks to Cyril MacDonald, Glace Bay, for his generous permission to use this photo from his Shedden Collection. Hand tinting by Grant Young.

Back Cover: Our thanks to Ken Schwartz, director of Two Planks and a Passion Theatre Company, for his photo of actors Chris O'Neill and Gordon Gammie.

Le Conseil des Arts du Canada | The Canada Council for the Arts

We acknowledge the support of the Canada Council for the Arts for our publishing program.

We also acknowledge support from Cultural Affairs, Nova Scotia Department of Tourism and Culture.

NOVA SCOTIA
Tourism and Culture

National Library of Canada Cataloguing in Publication Data

Melski, Michael, 1969-
Hockey mom, hockey dad : a play in two acts
1st ed.
ISBN 1-895415-68-3
I. Title.
PS8576.E477H62 2001 C812'.54 C2001-900558-X
PR9199.3.M429H62 2001

Hockey Mom, Hockey Dad

"Put me back in the game.
They need me."

—Ace Bailey,
after suffering critical brain injuries,
Dec.12, 1933 at Boston Garden.

Characters

DONNA in her late twenties.

TEDDY in his mid-thirties.

Place

An old hockey rink
on the outskirts of Sydney, Nova Scotia.

Time

Some Saturday mornings and Wednesday mornings, from September through February.

The Set

A section of bleachers and boards. There is no glass. The bleachers are littered and the paint is peeling. The boards are scratched up from a hundred years of scarring by pucks and sticks. A gate in the boards, near the blue line.

Note on Sound

A hockey "soundscape" is helpful for this play. The sound of skates struggling over ice; the shouts of excited children; the rousing of adult cheers. Hoarse, diehard voices in an old, mostly empty arena. This soundscape should be authentic, audible, but unobtrusive.

ACT I

A SATURDAY MORNING IN SEPTEMBER. Near the end of a game. As the lights rise on the section of bleachers, there are two parents near each other: DONNA and TEDDY. They are what they appear to be: two young, working class parents, watching their children play minor hockey.

DONNA is a few rows up from ice level in the bleachers. She is a quiet, modestly dressed young woman with pretty, unmade-up features. She holds a cup of coffee with both hands, warming them against the cold. Beside her is a newspaper.

TEDDY leans over the boards. He is a heavy-set, gregarious man, wearing an old hockey jacket. He lives the hockey action with fevered enthusiasm and body language, surging and sinking with every shot and play.

They are aware of each other's presence and proximity, but they don't know each other. Some of Teddy's volume is for Donna. Donna senses this, and is partly interested, partly unnerved by the attention. She regards Teddy, and the action on the ice, with some concern.

TEDDY: ...Faceoff! Everybody up! Okay now, take er out. Sticks on the ice! Heads-up plays, fellas. Only eight minutes left. Big comeback! BIG comeback! Can't let these Whalers beat us. Hustle down there, Troy, hustle for it! Stay left wing! Left! *(pause)* **Troy! Do ya know right from left or what? Jeez! LEFT! It's the hand ya wipe your nose with! Left!** *(pause)* **Ryan! Ya gotta go help my son. He's your man in the corner, Ryan! Fight him for it.... OWWW! Now what was that now?!**

A whistle blows.

Alright! Two minutes for holding! Good call, Ref! I take back everything I said about you and your sister. Okay boys...we got us a power play! Alright....

He looks up at the scoreboard.

...We're down by six and there's seven minutes left. Youse don't worry about that. Youse can still do it. That's...less than a goal a minute. Just gotta be positive! Okay! Change em up. Fresh legs, fellas. Let's go.

DONNA: Let's go, you guys.

Teddy sits down near her. He grins, tries to be nonchalant about it, but he's nervous as hell.

TEDDY: Looks like this one's a lost cause. Oh and Three. I think we got a losin streak on our hands.

Donna doesn't answer. He thrusts his arm at her. She starts.

I'm Teddy. I'm the loud guy ya always hear over there.

DONNA: Yeah. You are.

TEDDY: I thought I'd come over here today. See if the view was any better...here.

Silence between them.

DONNA: I don't think they should penalize the kids for holding. It'd be a lot nicer game if the players held each other more often.

pause

TEDDY: Yeah. That's very interestin. Hmm. What's your name?

He offers his hand again. She takes it, uneasy.

DONNA: Donna.

TEDDY: Hey. Donna. That's a pretty name.

DONNA: Thanks. *(at a loss)* **My mother picked it.**

TEDDY: I know it probly sounds like I'm hard on Troy. But ya gotta stay on him. The team gets down. He gives up too easy. He shouldn't give up so easy. He's a lot like his mother that way. My ex-wife. (*pause*) **Let's go guys! Not much of a power play! Stay sharp, Marco! Let's just break the shutout and make it dignified!**

DONNA: Go Leafs....

TEDDY: *(laughs)* **Well, they aren't gonna hear that from way over here, are they?**

She shrinks. Her next cheer is even smaller.

DONNA: Go Leafs....

TEDDY: So, uh...why do ya always sit over here by yourself? Past three weeks, ya been sittin by yourself, over here in no man's land.

DONNA: I...don't know anya the other parents.

TEDDY: Well, if ya want to get to know the people in

China, ya can't go sittin in Norway.

DONNA: Scuse me?

TEDDY: So is...ah...your husband not into the hockey?

DONNA: I'm...I'm not married. I don't have a husband.

TEDDY: Oh yeah. Ya don't say. Me neither. I don't got a husband either. I mean...well, you know what I mean.

Donna focuses on the game, uncertain of his company, and hesitant with all his personal questions.

DONNA: Let's go Leafs! C'mon.

TEDDY: *(shouts)* **C'mon Leafs! Leafs Leafs Leafs Leafs Leafs!**

DONNA: C'mon guys. You can do it.

TEDDY: So, which onea all these is yours?

pause

DONNA: Matthew. He's Number Four.

TEDDY: Oh! Number *Four*. So *you're* the one who owns Number Four!

DONNA: He's just a beginner. This is his first year playin.

TEDDY: Yeah. I noticed him. So your boy's a rookie, eh?

DONNA: Yeah. He's tryin to fit in. I guess all the

other kids were playin. My Matthew. He's....

She stops short.

TEDDY: What?

DONNA: Nothin. I'm talkin too much. I'm not like that. I never...talk this much.

TEDDY: Jeez. That's a lot, then.

She returns to the game.

C'mon. I finally got ya talkin a little to me. Don't go stoppin now. *(pause)* You're a quiet one. What are ya so nervous about?

DONNA: I'm just a little worried. About my kid. Y'know? I hope he can take carea himself out there. He's quiet. He's....

TEDDY: Y'know? What he needs is to put on more weight.

DONNA: *(taken aback)* Matthew's weight is normal for a boy his age. His weight is normal.

TEDDY: Sure, maybe it's normal for a boy his age who's takin piano lessons. But it's not normal for a boy his age who's a *defenceman.* Defencemen gotta stand up the forwards. They're tough.

DONNA: "Tough." Well, I guess I don't know much about that. I'm only his mother.

She turns back to the game, as it resumes. Teddy realizes he slipped.

TEDDY: He's got good instincts though. Very good instincts for defence.

pause

DONNA: He does?

TEDDY: Oh yeah. A lotta potential.

DONNA: How?

TEDDY: *(carefully)* **Well...like...he can skate backward...a few feet. He knows how to...ah...fall down in front of shots. Very important. Yeah, I can see. The potential in him. Yeah. A lotta potential....**

DONNA: *(beaming)* **Ya can? Really. No kiddin?**

TEDDY: Yeah. Definitely. I can see potential.

Teddy, undone by her smile, sees potential with her too.

DONNA: No ya can't. Can ya?

TEDDY: Yeah, yeah. I used to do a bitta coachin. I coached all these kids inthe Atom league.

DONNA: Y'know, cause, he's always surprisin me.

TEDDY: Well, I bet he could be a little Ray Bourque someday. With some trainin....

DONNA: Really. That's wonderful. *(pause)* **Who...?**

TEDDY: Hey, know what'd really help Matthew? Get him a bigger set of shoulder pads, fill him out some.

DONNA: Bigger shoulder pads?

TEDDY: Yeah. They got good ones down at Rudderham's. Really good protection. On special for only two hundred and change.

Donna sinks a little.

DONNA: I guess I'll have to go shake the money tree.

TEDDY: Yeah. With the registration, an the gear.... If Troy ever makes NHL, he owes me big time. He doesn't know it yet, but he's gonna have to buy me a condo in Florida.

DONNA: I had to tell Matthew. He could only either get Playstation or play hockey. I really couldn't afford either, but...your baby wants something. Ya dig deep for it.

TEDDY: Yep. I'm there. Rough, isn't it?

DONNA: I'll have to explain to him why Mom's turning tricks on the corner. To pay for his hockey equipment.

They laugh together.

TEDDY: I'd say Matt made a damn good call. Kids got a chance ta play outside, play real hockey, they should take it, insteada sittin inside exercisin their friggin thumbs.

DONNA: I'm not sure. Ya can't end up in a wheelchair for life from playin video hockey.

TEDDY: Hey. There he is! Number Four! Let's go

Matthew. C'mon, buddy!

They rise, moving closer to the action.

DONNA: Come on Matthew! Go get the puck. Watch out....

TEDDY: Don't screen your goalie, now. Heads up! Attaboy! Poke-check....

DONNA: Did you see? He touched the puck! WAY TO GO, MATTHEW! Ohhh...he fell.... Are you alright?! Matthew!

TEDDY: Get up, Matt! Get in there for it, buddy! C'mon. *(to her)* **He's gotta get in those corners more. He can't be scareda the corners.**

She leans over the boards.

DONNA: Be careful, sweetheart....

TEDDY: Go, Matt! Chase em down! Make him give it up! Don't be scaredcause he's big....

DONNA: *(screams)* **STAY OUTTA THE CORNERS, MATTHEW!**

Teddy is aghast.

TEDDY: Donna. Whattya tellin him that for?

DONNA: He can't....

TEDDY: Ya can't go tellin our defencemen to stay outta the corners. C'mon...!

DONNA: **He can't go in the corners with those shoulder pads! They're...cheap.**

A buzzer. The sound of cheering. Donna is just as exhausted as if she'd played the game herself.

TEDDY: **Another one down the toilet. Jeez. How do ya get your kid on a winnin team?**

DONNA: **It's a miracle no one got hurt out there.**

As the cheers die down, Teddy yells cross ice.

TEDDY: **Wait till next time you little Whaler goons! Are you ever gonna get the blubber stripped offa youse! We'll fix em, won't we, fellas? But first, next Saturday, we got a date with the Panthers, and there's gonna be a bounty on Panthers, eh? And then the next Saturday, we're gonna get the Jets! Right...? Right!**

DONNA: **I never expected the peewees ta play this rough.**

TEDDY: **Yeah. It might be house league but they play for keeps. They gotta learn that.**

DONNA: **But they're only eight years old. Attackin each other like that. They still look like babies ta me.**

TEDDY: *(laughs)* **It's alright. They got pads on. They're protected.**

Teddy jostles her playfully. She recoils, and rises. He follows suit.

The sound of a zamboni tractor is heard, approaching.

DONNA: Well. It was nice meeting....

TEDDY: So, ya gonna go down the dressin room to help Matthew with his gear?

DONNA: Uh. No.

TEDDY: Or ya just gonna wait up here for him to come out? What do ya usually do?

DONNA: I don't know. I usually...ah...I....

Donna, uncertain, wants to get away from him, and doesn't know what the right answer is.

TEDDY: What? Ya don't know what ya usually do?

DONNA: I usually...wait here.

TEDDY: Yeah. The dressin room ain't much fun after ya get smeared like this.

Teddy sits. She picks up her newspaper, opens to the classifieds, and determines to read.

So. What d'ya do anyways? Are ya workin now?

DONNA: *(not looking up)* **I'm a teacher. I been tryin to get some substitutin.**

TEDDY: A teacher! What a coincidence! Y'know, I'm the custodian over at Munroe High! So we're kinda in the same linea work, eh? More or less. Isn't that somethin?

DONNA: Yeah. More...or less.

She reads, wishing he would leave. He looks around the emptying arena.

TEDDY: This ol' rink. It's on its last legs. Some people think it oughta be condemned. The ice is slush. The bleachers. So old ya could fall through em places.

DONNA: Thanks, I'll tell Matthew. We'll be careful.

She tries again.

TEDDY: A lotta great memories in here, though. A lotta great memories.

DONNA: Really. Excuse me, I'm trying to....

TEDDY: I had my senior prom in this very rink. *(pause)* **I remember, up in the rafters there? There were these big pink clouds madea toilet paper. I went with my ex-wife, who wasn't my ex-wife then. We danced crazy. All night, under those friggin toilet paper clouds.** *(pause)* **Then we got married. And it rained shit.**

MUSIC starts to play softly from the arena loudspeakers.

DONNA: What's that music?

TEDDY: Oh. That's for the family skate. There's one booked in the rink every Saturday after the hockey. Boy. Now there's somethin I miss doin. Strappin on the old blades. Holdin hands....

Donna rises quickly, gathering her belongings.

DONNA: I think I better go over an find Matthew now.

TEDDY: Yeah?

DONNA: *(on her way out)* Yeah. Yeah....

TEDDY: Yeah. Can I say somethin? If I got too personal, y'know...I didn't mean...okay?

DONNA: What?

TEDDY: I mean, I know I come on strong. Do ya think I come on too strong?

DONNA: Well....

TEDDY: I just wanna say I'm sorry I mentioned "it." I know it makes me feel awful too. Bein here with all these couples. Whole families. Makes ya feel like shit, eh? *(pause)* Well...anyway, I'm sorry I mentioned it.

He moves to exit.

DONNA: It's okay. Ya just mentioned it. Ya didn't even know I was. Single, for sure.

TEDDY: Na. I could tell. I know, I just hate it sometimes when people mention "it" to me.

DONNA: Well. I won't mention "it" to you then.

TEDDY: *(laughs)* Okay, then, Donna. Thanks. I'll appreciate that.

pause

DONNA: Don't mention it.

They share a laugh.

very funny person.
it, I seen ya come in
.... *(pause)* Just
around, eh? I figured, I
efore one day I
...

ed in anythin right now.

one. I got a kid. I got

Sure. Yeah. Okay.

. Keepin me company.

n the lot waitin for me.

need help with his

on the front seat.
e window in by now.

ps him. He might be

eparate ways. The

music from the family skate is playing in the background

TEDDY: Uh. I bet I can probly find a set of Troy's old shoulder pads in the basement. If ya might want em for your Matthew. My little butterball...he outgrew em fast.

DONNA: I could pay ya. If you're sellin them.

TEDDY: Don't worry about that. I'll, uh, bring em to a practice or somethin.

DONNA: Okay. That's very kind. Thanks.

He exits.

TEDDY: Don't mention it. I'll see ya around.

Donna, alone with the music, looks out over the empty rink.

Scene 2

A practice. Teddy is chewing gum, leaning over the boards.

TEDDY: Get round those pylons. Pick it up Troy! Youse'r gonna have to keep doin this until ya get it right. You're never gonna knock off those Whalers with your good looks, so ya have to use hard work. Skate!

Donna enters behind him, this time wearing lipstick, and carrying a tin thermos of coffee.

DONNA: Hi.

TEDDY: *(forced offhand)* **Hey, you. Long time no see. Whatcha been up to?** *(back to ice)* **Boys, let's do it with a little more energy, eh? I know it's six-thirty in the morning, believe me, no one knows it better than your parents that have to sit here and watch youse be an insult to the great tradition of hockey. C'mon Dunner! I got a better chancea hittin the Six-Forty-Nine, than you got a scorin with that wimpy little shot.**

Donna lays out a small towel on the seat. She opens her coffee and pours a cup.

Yeah, yeah. Talk at me under your breath all ya want. Y'know, if I was still coachin youse, I'd trade the whole lotta ya for a few sticks and a bucketa Gatorade! Start over with kids from the tots league that don'twanna stay in the basement!

Teddy turns away, shaking his head.

DONNA: I hear we lost to the Panthers last week.

TEDDY: Ha. The zamboni only had to clear our halfa the ice. Someone shoulda brought a puck for *our* boys to play with.

He turns back to the practice.

DONNA: Matthew was kinda upset about it. He's really takin it seriously.

TEDDY: Yeah, that's good for him. He should be takin it seriously. At least Matt seems to take it serious. A lotta them out there think this is all for *fun* or somethin.

DONNA: Uh...?

TEDDY: Well, yeah, I know. I *know* it's for fun. But it's a lotta fun to win once in a while, in my opinion. At least, to have the remote possibility of winnin.

DONNA: Yeah. It'd be kinda nice to win a game. To see their faces.

pause

TEDDY: I brought the pads there. I been bringin them every game, practice for the last three weeks, but I ain't seen ya around.

DONNA: I just dropped Matthew off an picked him up after. Last coupla times. I got a seamstress job for last Saturday.

TEDDY: Oh. Ya weren't avoidin me, were ya? I thought ya might be avoidin me.

DONNA: Na. I wasn't avoidin ya....

TEDDY: Cause, I kinda took over your spot here. An then I didn't see ya around. *(pause)* C'mon fellas! Do it with a little heart, eh? C'mon...I can't tell the pylons from the players! Troy, you're the enforcer. So enforce a little, huh?

Teddy paces.

DONNA: What's wrong?

TEDDY: Five games in. We're already the friggin jokea the league. We gotta get this team motivated somehow. We're not hungry enough.

DONNA: Maybe the coach could take all the kids for ice cream. Ice cream is a great motivator. It always works wonders on Matthew.

He gives her a quizzical look.

Maybe we'll...get better as we go.

TEDDY: Not at this rate. Everything about this team sucks. Even our name is wrong.

DONNA: What's wrong with "Leafs?"

TEDDY: "Leafs." It's wimpy. That's what's wrong with it. It's a wet wimpy piece of plant. There's nothin more un-dangerous than a leaf.

DONNA: What about the Toronto Leafs?

TEDDY: Yeah, well, they suck too, lately. Just look at the other team names we play. There's the Panthers, the Jets, the Blazers....

DONNA: The Whalers....

TEDDY: An the Sharks. Now what do Sharks do ta Leafs? They eat them. Whalers...harpoon them. Blazers burn them. Panthers...crap on them. An Jets... crash into them. All a Leaf can do back to them is... flutter. That's why *Leafs* is a stupid name for a hockey team.

DONNA: It could be worse, though. What if they were called the Canadiens? Then the other teams could separate them. Ha ha....

Donna trails off, under Teddy's withering look.

TEDDY: I would just like Troy to be on a winner. I want him to have that experience of winnin. Not every game or nothin. Just, once in a while.

pause

DONNA: I'm just happy Matthew's out there. This is a big step for him.

He shouts.

TEDDY: Troy! If ever expect to make it to the NHL, ya better learn not to cheat your laps. Lift your arse up! If you're gonna be a grinder, ya still gotta be a skater too. Headsup Headsup! *(pause)* Jeez. I bet I got the fattest friggin kid in PeeWee.

DONNA: He's not that fat. He's just stocky.

TEDDY: Thanks, but stocky is just a polite way of sayin "porky." *(laughs)* I got him trainin, on a workout schedule. But he likes eatin too much. Just like me. I love him though. He's the only good thing I got left.

Donna is moved, in spite of herself, by Teddy's softness.

DONNA: So, Troy wants to play in the NHL some day.

TEDDY: Sure does. But he gotta get his weight down. And, he gotta be on a winnin team. He can't go anywhere upwards in hockey unless he gets outta this crappy house league an onto the rep teams. The rep teams are the best players in league. An the rep coach never scouts the basement lookin for the talent.

DONNA: And we're in the basement.

TEDDY: Oh yeah. Yeah. I'd say we're more like in a little dark corner of the basement. So we gotta win some games. We gotta get the rep coach out here. We gotta get his attention. That's how it happens. That's how it happened with Al McInnis from the Blues. Bobby Smith. Mike McPhee. They all made it from here. Al McInnis is from friggin Port Hood, for Jesus' sakes. Port Hood!

pause

DONNA: I guess it is possible. Isn't it?

TEDDY: Al McInnis! 'Eighty-eight Stanley Cup Conn Smythe trophy! From Port Hood! Port Hood is nowhere. Port Hood is like...the Flin Flon, Manitoba of Cape Breton. If he can do it, that means it can be done. He's an NHL hero now.

DONNA: *(more to self)* **A hero....**

TEDDY: Yeah. He got their attention. Ya just gotta get someone's attention.

DONNA: I guess ya do. That's for sure.

He watches the practice.

TEDDY: I figure every team needs an enforcer. Y'know? Ya got guys like Tie Domi, Dave Semenko...they made it. They're no Brett Hulls. I mean, I know I got a chubby kid. I figure as long as he can skate a little with them, he might just have a place up there. *(shouts)* **Alright Troy! When you go into the**

corners on this drill, start passin out elbow sandwiches! And you don't let anybody give you no flak! If they do, you just...sit on them! That's it! *(fiery)* **HIT EM HARD!...**

Donna rises quickly.

DONNA: I'm gonna pay ya for these pads, y'know.

TEDDY: What? Are ya leavin now?

DONNA: I said, I'm gonna pay ya. For these shoulder pads. How much?

TEDDY: Just tell Matt they're a present. From Troy's dad.

DONNA: Thanks, but I don't need charity, okay? We're gettin along fine.

TEDDY: Hey, I wasn't sayin anythin about charity. I just know....

DONNA: Ya don't know anythin about me. Ya don't even know us.

TEDDY: Well. I know you're kinda worried about your Matt...bein protected.

DONNA: *(suddenly)* **Would ya stop callin him Matt? Don't call him Matt! He's not a Matt!**

TEDDY: Huh?

DONNA: His name is Matthew. That's his christened name. He's not a Matt.

TEDDY: Alright. He's not a Matt, then. Jeez Louise....

DONNA: Matt's are somethin...ya step on. Somethin... ya throw on a floor!

TEDDY: What's goin on anyway? Why are ya grossin me out?

DONNA: Do ya see "Welcome" written on him anywhere? Do ya?

TEDDY: No, Donna. I don't see welcome written on him.

DONNA: No? Good.

TEDDY: I don't see it written on his mom, either. That's for sure. That's for damn sure.

Teddy turns his back.

Donna stops. Considers.

DONNA: *(softer)* Hey....

TEDDY: Look, I can deal with bein grossed out. But I'd like to know what I did, eh?

DONNA: It's just...his father calls him Matt. He called him Matt all the time. He was Matthew's...hero. What ya said before.

pause

TEDDY: Jeez. You're shakin....

DONNA: I'm fine. I shouldn't've....

TEDDY: Your hands are shakin like crazy. Ya been drinkin all that coffee.

DONNA: I'm cold, that's why. We're in a rink, y'know.

TEDDY: If you're cold, I'm gonna give ya my mitts.

DONNA: Then your hands'll get cold. I don't want your mitts.

TEDDY: Tell ya what. I'll give ya one, and I'll keep one.

DONNA: Look, I really don't need....

TEDDY: Hey, Donna. They amputate for frostbite, y' know.

She laughs a little, and lets him put the glove on her hand.

DONNA: They should amputate my tongue. For spillin my guts like that to someone I barely know. Just the other day, I only met ya once.

TEDDY: Stop me if I go offside, okay? How long has it been for?

DONNA: "It?"

TEDDY: *(laughs)* Yeah. "It."

DONNA: We split about a year an a half ago. After eight an a half years. *(pause)* I'm sorry. I know it's not polite to do this.

TEDDY: Not polite to do what?

DONNA: Just to talk about your ex ta other people. That's what I read, I think.

TEDDY: Oh yeah. An where did ya read that, now?

DONNA: I don't know. I think it was in a *Chatelaine*. At Matthew's doctor's office.

TEDDY: Oh. Was it onea those articles about how to meet people? How to find that special someone...?

DONNA: Yeah. Y'know, they're everywhere.

TEDDY: So I thought ya told me ya weren't interested in anythin right now?

silence

DONNA: I'm not.

TEDDY: Oh yeah. So why were ya readin an article like that, then? Hmm?

DONNA: It was just a magazine. That's all. It didn't mean nothin.

TEDDY: Ah. I see. You opened it to the "love chapter" by accident....

DONNA: Pediatrician kept him waitin three hours, it was either read magazines or Mother Goose, for God sakes!

A whistle blast.

DONNA: Here. I better give ya your mitt back. I don't wanna leave with it.

He takes her hand as she tries to take it off.

TEDDY: I gotta question for ya. Here it is. Do ya like ice skatin?

DONNA: Teddy....

TEDDY: That's me. Cuddly, and good to take to bed.

DONNA: I bet ya don't use that one much, do ya.

TEDDY: Ya didn't answer my question. Do ya like ice skatin? Yes or no.

Donna doesn't respond. Teddy becomes dramatic.

Quick. The clock's tickin down. She's barely got time, the crowd's goin crazy...they're on their feet, chantin..."See Teddy...See Teddy...Date Teddy, Date Teddy...!" Quick! What's the answer?! Ya like ice skatin or what?

DONNA: *(flustered)* **Yeah. I like ice skatin.**

TEDDY: Good. Then we'll go on a family skate. Whaddya say? My treat.

DONNA: No. Can ya let goa my hand?

TEDDY: What hand?

DONNA: My hand. The one you're holdin now.

TEDDY: Oh. You're mistaken. I'm not holdin your hand. I'm holdin my mitt. Your hand just happens to be in it.

DONNA: Maybe you should hold something else.

She pulls away without the glove.

TEDDY: I'm pretty sure ya like me. I think ya do. After the other time, I was sure ya didn't.

pause

DONNA: Sure. I...like ya....

TEDDY: But, it's like ya don't want to like me. C'mon. Just gimme a chance.

Donna shakes her head.

Two longer whistle blasts.

DONNA: Here they come.

TEDDY: They sure don't look much like a packa killers, do they?

DONNA: Na. I guess they don't.

pause

TEDDY: Y'know, though? Every once in a while out there, there's a flash of somethin.

DONNA: Pardon?

pause

TEDDY: I mean, like a flash of magic happenin out there. Some kid ya neverknew had it. Just all of sudden, they're beautiful to watch. Everything works for them.

DONNA: Yeah?

TEDDY: Yeah. Somethin, somewhere...clicks. They come outta nowhere. Unstoppable. They're like a comet, sailin. Some kid...destined for somethin really special. *(pause)* **Ya never know when. Ya never know who.**

DONNA: I guess ya never know, do ya?

silence

TEDDY: It really happens. Just right out there....

Their shoulders are touching. Donna bristles a little. But she does not move away.

Scene 3

Two weeks later. A buzzer sounds. Mid-game. Teddy leaning over, speaking to Troy, unseen, a short distance away on the ice. Donna sitting behind, drinking from her thermos of coffee.

TEDDY: Troy! Alright, I don't haveta tell ya, do I? That was a pretty stinkin first period, wasn't it? Yeah, I know they got a good goalie. *(pause)* **Don't go gettin mad at her cause she's a girl. She's the best friggin player on the ice right now, ya weiner. Alright, when Adam gets set up for the big shot, I want ya to get in the crease with her...just move in there with her, set up housekeepin. An get that stick between her pads to keep her off balance. Got it?**

DONNA: *(quietly)* **That's called "goaltender interference."**

He gives her a look.

TEDDY: Well, aren't you the smart one today? *(back to ice)* **Troy, I know ya don't wanna get a penalty. But sometimes ya have to, ya gotta send this goalie a message. She might be built like Ken Dryden, but we aren't gonna treat her like no Hall of Famer, are we? This is hockey, an if she's gonna play with boys, she's gonna have to....** *(pause)* **Hey, I don't care what ya seen on Coaches' Corner. This! This right here where your dad is? This is Coaches' Corner.** *(pause)* **Troy, c'mon now! I'm just sayin get in the crease with her. I'm not askin ya to kiss her on the mouth!**

A whistle blasts. Teddy speaks over his shoulder as he walks up the bleachers.

You watch, then. Don't listen to me. That goalie's like a female second cominga that Russian guy...Tretiak! *(to Donna)* **We're gonna befriggin Oh and Seven, after this game...** *(back to ice)* **an if you an the resta them'd listen, we could be Seven an Oh instead. Go ahead! Play the game your way. Don't listen to Dad. Go be a weiner! I bet ya she shuts youse out cold. I bet she's in the pros before any of ya.**

Teddy moves to sit beside Donna.

DONNA: Don't sit on my coffee, Teddy! God, the last thing I need this mornin is the taste of your arse in my cuppa coffee.

TEDDY: Ya know, that's probly why you're in such a crappy mood today. Ya drink a lotta coffee, ya know.

DONNA: Well. You say "friggin" a lot. So get offa my back.

TEDDY: Jeez. I think I liked it better those days when ya weren't talkin to me.

DONNA: Don't ya ever get the message about anythin? Don't ya? Are ya stupid?

TEDDY: Hey. Are you gonna talk civil to me this period? Or is it gonna be like the first period? *(pause)* What? Are ya mad at me because I called ya at home? What's the big...?

DONNA: I just wanna know how....

TEDDY: The coach gave it to me. I told him we were sharin drives.

DONNA: Ya never said anythin to me about sharin drives!

TEDDY: Well do ya wanna share drives? We can share drives if ya want to share drives. That'd be great.

DONNA: The coach gave it to ya. Why does he think people go outta their way an pay to get unlisted numbers?

TEDDY: Come on, Donna. He sees us together. Everyone sees us together.

DONNA: Well, we aren't "together." They got no right....

TEDDY: I know we aren't "together." I know. Believe me, I know.

pause

DONNA: What did ya want anyway? Did ya call about sharin drives? Was it really that?

TEDDY: If you'da let me talk a bit, insteada runnin to save Matthew from drownin in the tub. Yeah, an eight year old kids really drown in the bathtub. Good one.

DONNA: They *do*. What did ya call me for?

TEDDY: I was down at Muzzie's havin some beers... someone offered me two tickets to a Screamin Eagles game. Troy was with his mom someplace. I didn't want to waste two Eagle tickets on a guy, so, called ya. That's all.

DONNA: I wouldn't gone with ya.

TEDDY: Well, I wouldn't called ya. Except they were playin the Mooseheads. An it was probly gonna be a good game!

pause

DONNA: Well ya can't call me. Don't call me again.... Okay?

TEDDY: Why can't I call ya? We could car pool. We could really car pool.

DONNA: I told ya. I don't even know ya that well.

TEDDY: What don't ya know? What do ya need to know? I'll tell ya.

DONNA: I just don't know ya. I don't want to know ya.... Okay?!

pause

TEDDY: Hey. Just cause a guy goes out of his way to find your number doesn't mean he's a friggin...Teddy Bundy or somethin. He might just like ya...an...I do....

DONNA: Just don't call me, okay? Please. It just makes it harder.

TEDDY: Alright then. I'll never call ya again. Okay? If that's what ya want, for sure. But if ya ever want ta share drives, I'm in the book.

Silence. They watch the game.

DONNA: He...was callin me for awhile. Callin me up long distance. That's why I gotta spend for the unlisted number.

pause

TEDDY: What was he sayin to ya?

DONNA: He's the kinda guy who calls ya collect to make obscene phone calls. Worst thing is, I'm the kinda person who accepts the charges. Here she goes again. That must be what you're thinkin, eh.

TEDDY: So...what are ya tellin me? You still got feelings for your ex. That's why you don't want to know me. Okay. I get it.

pause

DONNA: No. Ya don't.

TEDDY: Then what?

There is a sound of cheering.

DONNA: **What happened? Something just happened.**

TEDDY: **Jeez, I haven't even been followin it.**

DONNA: **I just saw the end of it over your shoulder.**

TEDDY: **We scored! Must've been Adam.***(shouts)* **Way ta go, Leafs! Great goal, buddiiees!** *(pause)* **Now we're only down by three, anyways. That's pretty good for second periods this year.**

DONNA: **I think...it was Troy. I think.**

silence

TEDDY: **Na. Couldn'ta been. Troy's not a scorer.**

DONNA: **I think.... Look, he's still got his stick up in the air.**

Teddy scans the ice. He looks faint.

TEDDY: **My boy...scored?**

DONNA: *(shouts)* **Good goal, Troy! Good work!**

TEDDY: **Holy...Holy shit...ah....**

DONNA: **Way to go, Troy! Go Leafs....**

TEDDY: **Troy...Holy....**

DONNA: **Attaboy, Troy!**

TEDDY: **Holy Holy HOT steaming SHIT! MY BOY**

SCORED A GOAL!

DONNA: Good shot...!

Teddy does a spontaneous dance.

TEDDY: *(chants)* **My boy scored a goal! My boy scored a goal! My boy scored a goal!**

DONNA: *(laughs)* **Be careful, you're gonna break through the bleachers.**

TEDDY: An...an...I didn't even see it! His first goal. His first friggin GOAL. What? How? How did it happen? Did ya see it? What happened? Tell me what happened!

The game resumes.

DONNA: I think it was a rebound.

TEDDY: My God, what a beautiful rebound! *(shouts)* **What a beautiful rebound!**

DONNA: Teddy. Everyone's lookin over at ya....

TEDDY: *(ecstatic)* **So? Who cares. I got somethin to be proud of this time! I LOVE YA, TROY! Just wait till the rep coach gets a loada him. My little butterball scored...a real goal.**

DONNA: He sure did.

TEDDY: On a beautiful, gorgeous, delectible rebound. Just...just like I coached him to. He musta parked himself. An it worked? What I said worked. On that hot shit goalie they got...it actually worked!

DONNA: That's the first goal they scored on her. She's good.

TEDDY: *(shouts at the goalie)* **HEY! How do ya like THEM apples, Madame Vladislav Friggin Tretiak!** *(roars with laughter)* **Go back to the minors, with ya, eh?**

DONNA: Teddy. This *is* the minors.

TEDDY: *(to the goalie)* **Hope they don't send ya off to SIBERIA or nothin!**

DONNA: *(laughs)* **Hey, this ain't Russia. They don't even do that in Russia anymore.**

TEDDY: I don't care! I don't care what the hell they do over in Russia!

Teddy suddenly takes her face in his hands and kisses her.

She is shocked. He is shocked as well.

A buzzer sounds.

silence

DONNA: Good...good shift, guys.

TEDDY: Yeah...good shift! Great stuff, Troy...we showed em, didn't we?

DONNA: Way to go...good shift.

TEDDY: You get out there next shift an score again. You're no Yzerman yet, buddy...eh?

DONNA: Good job...Leafs.

TEDDY: ...Yeah...don't you sit on the bench there now an start smellin your own farts.

DONNA: Good shift...! Good....

TEDDY: Good shift...yeah....

DONNA: Good....

TEDDY: Shift....

They look at each other.

A whistle. Game play resumes.

TEDDY: Sorry about that. I...I kinda....

DONNA: It's...okay.

TEDDY: ...Got carried away, y'know. It was...the heat of the moment. I shouldn'ta....

DONNA: ...It's okay.

TEDDY: He just...never scored before, I can't.... *(pause)* **It is? Okay?**

DONNA: Yeah. I mean....

TEDDY: You're not cross at me?

DONNA: Yeah. No...I mean no. Just...you can forget it.

pause

TEDDY: Come ice skatin with me. Come to an Eagles game. Come to Muzzie's with me.

DONNA: I can't. I told ya. I keep tellin ya.

TEDDY: Come anywhere with me. Come ice skatin. Okay?

DONNA: I can't ice skate.

TEDDY: I can teach ya. I used to be a coach, remember?

DONNA: I can ice skate. I just...can't anymore.

TEDDY: Why? Do ya need skates? I can find ya a paira skates. I know lots people got skates.

DONNA: I broke up my knee before.

TEDDY: Oh. It's an injury.

DONNA: Yeah. I tore some ligaments. Fallin down some stairs when I was little.

TEDDY: When ya were little? So, the doctor, he told ya, ya couldn't ever skate anymore?

DONNA: No. But....

TEDDY: Then it's healed by now. Donna, you're not gonna fall.

DONNA: Teddy. Ice is...slippery. *(pause)* I can't go skatin with ya. I can't go anywhere with anybody right now.

Teddy turns her around gently, makes her look at him.

TEDDY: **Why do ya want to be alone like this. Why would anyone want to be?**

DONNA: **I got Matthew. He's...we're not alone. We're never alone.**

TEDDY: **Y'know what? I'm a family man. It's simple, I know. It's not very ambitious, I guess. I want to have a family again. I think there's nothin more, nothin better ya can do than start a family.**

DONNA: **That's a laugh.**

TEDDY: **How is that a laugh?**

DONNA: **Any guy with a zipper can start a family. It's not a very hard thing to do.**

TEDDY: **That's not what I meant. You know that. I'm not good at expressin very well.** *(pause)* **I would like us to be a couple. I know I'm not much. What you're lookin at, this is it, y'know.**

DONNA: **Is it?** *(more to herself)* **Why take the chance? If I stay alone, I don't get hurt. I don't need anya that now.**

pause

TEDDY: **Hey. Ya ever get up in the mornin, some winter mornin. Look out the window an see the trees all covered with ice? And they're hangin over with the weight of it, but it's the most amazing sculpture?**

(pause) This day last year, I was gettin up, makin Troy his breakfast. I tried to talk a bit to him, but he had his face fulla pancakes. So, I sat by myself in fronta the window, started tapin his sticks. It musta rained an froze the night before. I was lookin at those trees. At the...beauty of them. An I didn't have anyone I could share it with. *(pause)* Troy's sticks had about eight layersa tape each on the blades. A chainsaw couldn'ta nicked em.

pause

DONNA: What are ya buggin me for, Teddy? Why are ya pickin on me? You gotta tell me...why ya like me. An ya gotta be honest. Can ya be?

TEDDY: Well. You're pretty foxy. That's one thing.

DONNA: I might've known you'd go for the physical first....

TEDDY: *(teases)* Well, you know me. I play the body....

DONNA: This body can't take much more. I'm twenty-nine goin on fifty-nine. An for your information, I'm ugly as sin. So I know you're lying already.

TEDDY: I'd say you're gorgeous.

DONNA: No I'm not. An I'm not too bright either. Why do ya think I can't get a teachin job? I got no guts. I'm not brave at all. I'm broke. I got nothing to offer a guy.

TEDDY: Alright. You tell me. Why do you think I like ya?

pause

DONNA: Cause. I'm a single mom. I'm a pushover. I'm as desperate as it gets.

TEDDY: *(very simple)* No. I think you're a very strong person. An I thinkyou're a beautiful...mother.

silence

DONNA: Well, that...doesn't say much for you then. Ya got such bad taste.

TEDDY: You're beautiful.

DONNA: I gotta go now. I...I wasn't supposed to stay this long.

TEDDY: Donna. Are ya cryin?

DONNA: No. I'm not cryin. I got some dust in my eye. From the ceilin?

TEDDY: Do ya? Here....

She rises quickly and moves to exit.

DONNA: This rink's fallin down. It oughta be condemned. It's dangerous.

TEDDY: What about the game? What about Matthew? Ya can't leave.

DONNA: Could...could ya maybe...do a favour for me?

TEDDY: Sure. Anythin. What is it?

DONNA: I got a job. Doin some dressmakin to bring in some extra money. There's not much teachin. I'm on the top of the list for a pregnancy leave, but....

TEDDY: No one's pregnant. Need me ta get some teachers pregnant for ya?

pause

DONNA: Very funny. I gotta go finish this dress by noon. The lady who owns it wants it for tonight.

TEDDY: Sure. I'll take Matthew home for ya. No problem.

DONNA: I wouldn't leave him. I'd never ask ya, but....

TEDDY: I'd love to do that for ya. Anytime. You name it.

DONNA: Could ya take him to Kate's for an ice cream after maybe? If I give ya some money?

TEDDY: I won't take any money for that.

DONNA: He loves goin for ice cream after the games. I know it's almost winter.

TEDDY: I'll take him for chicken, too. Me an Troy always go for fried chicken.

DONNA: Fried chicken. At this hour of the morning? It's ten-thirty.

TEDDY: Yeah. We usually get the first batch they make. *(laughs)* I love it too. I'll take Matthew.

pause

DONNA: Matthew said Troy was kinda teasin him. About the shoulder pads, y'know? How kids are about hand-me-downs?

TEDDY: You don't worry about that. That won't happen again.

DONNA: I wouldn't even say nothin, but....

TEDDY: *(laughs)* They'll get along like a house on fire. Trust me. Or Troy'll have a little arse on fire.

DONNA: No. Don't get mad at him. Forget I said it.

TEDDY: Hey, c'mon. I'm kiddin.

She starts to leave.

DONNA: Be careful with him, okay? Be sure he buckles up. He's got a key....

TEDDY: Don't worry. I'll take real good care of him. It's my pleasure. Anythin to help.

DONNA: I really, really appreciate it.

TEDDY: Well, you're welcome.

She summons her courage and swiftly kisses his mouth.

DONNA: I'll see ya, okay? I'll see ya later.

The game continues. Teddy, stunned, watches her leave. Then he begins to sing and dance and shout, daring the bleachers to break.

He dances till he is exhausted. Then he lifts up her silver coffee thermos, hoisting it high, as if it were the Stanley Cup.

TEDDY: I love this friggin game...!

A buzzer sounds

END OF ACT I

ACT 2

BEFORE A PRACTISE, about three weeks later. Donna and Teddy are sharing the same blanket. They drink out of identical mugs, with the remains of half-eaten muffins on the seats beside them. Donna is wearing a poppy.

DONNA: Go Leafs. Go Leafs....

TEDDY: *(louder)* **Go Leafs!** *(pause)* **Leafs Leafs Leafs Leafs!**

DONNA: Go Leafs! Leafs Leafs Leafs Leafs!

TEDDY: Leafs Leafs Leafs Leafs...!

DONNA: Leafs Leafs Leafs Leafs Leafs!

pause

TEDDY: C'mon, Donna. It's for the team. The Moms an Dads are part of the team.

DONNA: It sounds silly, though. It sounds like we're cheerin for "sleeves."

TEDDY: *(chants)* **Go Leafs Go! Go Leafs Go! Go Leafs Go!...**

DONNA: Why are ya makin me do this? The kids aren't even out on the ice yet. Besides, it's not even a game. It's only a practice....

TEDDY: *(laughs)* Well, that's what we gotta do. Practice. The fans have to practice too.

DONNA: I'm too shy to be a good fan. I don't even like yellin when I'm in a classroom.

He sits down beside her.

TEDDY: Alright then. We're gonna get the wave. Once an for all. Ready?

DONNA: No way. No more waves, Teddy.

TEDDY: I'm not lettin ya give up on the wave. I know we can get the wave.

DONNA: We're un-coordinated. *I'm* un-coordinated.

TEDDY: Listen. Two people can do one wave. It can't be that difficult. If a person can do two things at once....

DONNA: It's jinxed.

TEDDY: It's not jinxed. If a person can walk an chew gum, crap an read the paper, then two people can easily do one wave.

DONNA: Alright. One more try. One more. An that's it.

She grins, exasperated. They get set and count down together.

TEDDY: One...two...three....

DONNA: One...two...three....

Teddy does a graceful wave. Donna stays seated.

TEDDY: Why didn't ya do it that time? What happened?

DONNA: I was watchin yours. *(laughs)* **It was such a good one.**

Teddy kisses her. She kisses back, but doesn't give herself totally.

DONNA: There's people here now. The other parents. The kids are cominout on the ice.

Pause

TEDDY: I want...more than this. I'm gonna need more than this.

DONNA: I know.

TEDDY: Why won't ya come anywhere with me? We're goin out, but we don't "go out."

DONNA: I told ya. I need to go slow.

TEDDY: But, I want ya to come places with me. I been waitin a long time to do these things. I want ya to come to Muzzie's with me. I want ya to let me buy ya fancy drinks an we could dance a bit. I want to watch the boys spit up their nachos when ya come in holdin my hand.

DONNA: That'd be fun to watch, wouldn't it. I think maybe I'd rather a movie instead.

TEDDY: Fine. A movie, then. Let's go to the video store together. Ya coulda come last Sunday with us.

DONNA: I just have to get used to all of this. It takes time.

TEDDY: How much time? I can't wait forever. I like ya so much.

DONNA: Teddy. I like you, too. But the last time I was single for any lengtha time was a long time ago. An I didn't have Matthew then. Maybe it's easier for you. This is my top speed right now. I can't go any faster.

pause

TEDDY: Well. This is real fast then. Whoosh. The coyote could never catch you, could he? Slow down, you're makin me dizzy! Hey, Rocket, two minutes for lookin so good.

Donna tries to smile. They watch the practice in silence.

He puts his arm cautiously around her. They try to get comfortable—his arm around her waist, arm around shoulder. Finally, they settle on holding hands.

DONNA: Matthew seems to really like ya. He told me you took he an Troy out trainin Sunday.

TEDDY: Yeah. We did a little roadwork. Took some shots. Nothin too heavy. He's a real bright little fella. Let me spend a little time with him, I'll show him how to play the game.

DONNA: *(teasing)* You mean, you'll make him not-so-

bright anymore? *(pause)* **Ya really do like Matthew, don't ya, Teddy?**

TEDDY: Of course I do. I like him a lot. I love to see him goin for it. Even more, I'd like if his mom would go for it....

Donna is a little uncomfortable, evades his amorous advance and changes the subject.

DONNA: So. What movie did youse end up gettin? When he stayed for supper Sunday.

TEDDY: Uh, what movie?

DONNA: Yeah, I forget to ask him about it. I was sewing all day.

TEDDY: Oh. I remember. I rented them the Child's Play movies. A double header.

DONNA: Ya didn't. Ya did?

TEDDY: Yeah. Those were the ones they brought over. He an Troy. They wanted them.

pause

DONNA: *(angry)* **I told you, Teddy. I don't want him watchin those horror movies.**

TEDDY: They're not horror movies. It's just that little "Chucky" guy. They're popular movies.

DONNA: Don't let him get any horror movies. I asked ya....

TEDDY: They're not horror movies anyways. They're more like comedies. They're funny. They make ya laugh.

DONNA: It makes ya laugh when a little kid's puppet goes around stabbin people?

TEDDY: *(laughs)* Donna. It's a movie. It's only a movie, for Jesus' sakes. Calm down.

DONNA: Matthew still watches Sesame Street....

TEDDY: Hey. Don't ya think he's a little old for that? Sesame Street. I mean, he's eight....

DONNA: I teach little kids. They can't distinguish.... He's not too old for Sesame Street...!

TEDDY: Well, I teach little kids too. An I think ya gotta let the boy grow upa little.

DONNA: Well, I don't want him thinkin that Grover is gonna come after...Big Bird with a butcher knife. Kids don't know....

TEDDY: *(laughs)* Listen to ya! Did ya hear what ya just said? I think you're bein a little foolish here, now....

pause

DONNA: Don't make fun of me! The way I'm raisin my son.... Ever! He's nothin to you!

pause

TEDDY: *(quietly)* He's not nothin to me.

silence

They watch the practice.

He pours her more coffee. She takes it.

DONNA: I just get a little scared. Matthew's into this game so much. It's all he talks about now.

TEDDY: Don't ya think the game's good for him?

DONNA: I wonder what he's gonna take home. From all this bumpin, an swearin, an slashin at each other. The other night, I was tuckin him in bed and he cross-checked me with his pillow. It was only a pillow, he was just showin me how to do it, but...that doesn't seem too normal to me.

TEDDY: Sure it is. Just means he's getting "hooked."

Teddy laughs at his pun. Donna doesn't.

DONNA: Sometimes, I think it's a great thing. That he's bein so physical...an assertin himself. An learnin to get along. An then, other times....

TEDDY: Hey. Let me tell ya somethin. Let me show ya somethin about contact sports. Okay?

DONNA: What?

He steps down the bleachers to the gate in the boards.

TEDDY: Contact sports help kids...help people to get their frustrations out. So they got an outlet, right? An outlet for them, like in electrics. So they don't short-

circuit, go on a shootin spree an kill everyone at the Wal-Mart or somethin.

Teddy opens the gate in the boards and steps out onto the ice.

DONNA: Teddy. What are ya doin? Ya can't go out on the ice.

TEDDY: ...So if they want to hit each other, which is somethin a lotta kids want to do by *nature*, then they can do it with expensive pads on. So they don't really hurt themselves. See?

DONNA: I think ya should get offa the ice. They're practisin.

TEDDY: They're way down there havin a huddle. Don't worry about it. Come on down.

DONNA: No way. Thanks anyway.

TEDDY: Anyway, that's the lesson. *(laughs)* **Class dismissed.**

He slips on the ice, and takes a header.

That...that wasn't parta the lesson.

DONNA: *(laughs)* **Are ya sure it doesn't hurt hittin that ice?**

TEDDY: It's worth it if I can make ya laugh. I love ya when ya laugh.

They both realize he came close to saying he loves her.

Teddy starts back up.

DONNA: Teddy. How do you get your frustrations out? What's your...outlet?

TEDDY: Well. I think about you. *(laughs)* **...Who is the sourcea most of them. But, I gotta give credit to our team too, this season bein pure hell.**

pause

DONNA: What do ya think about me?

TEDDY: I think how perfect we could be. If we got together. Really together. *(pause)* **I ain't gettin any younger. I need for dreams to start coming true now. I know we could be...a real good team.**

Donna thinks. A dreamy, but tentative look in her eyes.

DONNA: Even if we can't do the wave together?

TEDDY: One more time. Let's break the curse.

DONNA: One more try. Alright.

As Teddy and Donna do the perfect wave, there is a LIGHTING CHANGE.

Scene 5

When the lights come back up on Donna and Teddy, they are older, in voice and gesture, as if twenty years had passed.

It is the Stanley Cup Finals. The last bars of the National Anthem are heard. Donna and Teddy stand patriotically.

DONNA: Here we are. I can hardly believe it.

TEDDY: Me neither. The Stanley Cup Finals. Our boys...!

DONNA: This is a dream, isn't it?

TEDDY: ...The Stanley Cup Finals. In Toronto!

DONNA: Alright. So this is a dream.

TEDDY: Yeah, but it's a great one. Look at them out there. Big stars. Ron McLean came up and actually *asked* for my opinion.

DONNA: And you wore out the poor man's microphone giving it to him.

TEDDY: Early retirement. No more cleaning strange graffiti off bathroom walls. Life's a vacation.

DONNA: Matthew's married to some blond girl from California. They look great together. They've both had plastic surgery.

TEDDY: Troy's got an endorsement with KFC. We're in chicken heaven. They even *deliver*.

DONNA: Matthew's taking creatine. He says not to worry, it's just like vitamins. I don't get it. Why can't he just chew Flintstones?

Music begins. "We are the Champions." Teddy and Donna are euphoric.

TEDDY: WE WON!

DONNA: WE WON THE STANLEY CUP!

TEDDY: All my life I wanted them to drink from the same cup, that Gordie Howe, and Belliveau, and Lafleur and Gretzky....

DONNA: I just hope they sterilize that thing once in a while.

Teddy leans over and kisses her. They begin to slow dance in the bleachers.

TEDDY: Didn't we make those beautiful children what they are?

DONNA: Maybe. I guess maybe we did make a good team.

TEDDY: Laying newspapers on the kitchen floor so they could eat with their skates on.

DONNA: It was like living in a giant litterbox.

TEDDY: Only a beautiful mom could have such patience.

DONNA: Only a *demented* mom. And a dreaming dad.

The music starts to fade away. Their voices start to fade along with it.

TEDDY: So what's wrong with dreaming?

DONNA: Nothing. Except the waking-up part.

A referee's whistle breaks the illusion.

The lights snap hard back to REALITY.

Scene 6

Two weeks later. Donna and Teddy are in the bleachers, leaning over the boards, pleading with Matthew to get up off the ice. Matthew isn't moving.

TEDDY: C'mon Matthew. Just stand up. That's all you gotta do. They can't start play again until you stand your little self up.

DONNA: Matthew. It's not your fault they scored.

TEDDY: Yeah. That's what mistakes are for. *(pause)* **Tell you what. Teddy'll get you an ice cream if you can just skate back to the bench over there.**

DONNA: Baby. You're gonna get sick if you sit on that ice....

TEDDY: Let's go. Hop to it, before your bum cheeks freeze together.

DONNA: Teddy. He doesn't need to be scared. He needs to take his time.

TEDDY: We don't got much time. We'll get a delay-of-game penalty. We're already down four zip. *(to Troy)* Troy! Go pick up Matthew! Troy...where you goin? *(pause)* No, Troy! You're not going to the canteen in the middle of the game! You need another hot dog like you need measles! *(with emphasis)* Go-pick-up-Matthew!

Troy responds. There is a burst of applause.

Donna steps back, embarrassed.

DONNA: I don't know what's wrong. He's doing so well, but he just, withdraws sometimes. He keeps falling down.

TEDDY: I'll tell ya his whole problem. It's his skates. They gotta be sharpened. I looked at em, an they ain't been sharpened all season. He can't move out there.

pause

DONNA: I know. We keep forgettin to do it. To get them sharpened....

TEDDY: He ain't gonna go anywhere playin this game if he's got dull skates on. An nonea that happy coachie horseshit is gonna do any good if he doesn't got at least a fightin chance to play along with these kids.

DONNA: I know. I know....

TEDDY: What? I'm just tryin to tell ya. Why he's gettin frustrated.

DONNA: *(blurts)* I was just waitin till I got the power bill cleared up. That's all. I didn't mean to hurt his chances. I know it's only like five bucks to get them sharpened. But...we just have to cut to the essentials some times. For a little bit anyway. I mean I figured, what's the sense of him gettin pneumonia? If they shut our power off. I figured, as long as he's not cold at home, then his skates, my take-out coffees, they could wait a bit. I didn't know...they couldn't....

TEDDY: Why didn't ya *tell* me? I woulda done it for ya easy. I take Troy's skates in every week.

DONNA: I didn't know. They couldn't wait. I can barely get the car started twice in a row to get him here....

TEDDY: That's why you should come and stay with me. We'll get him here. Together. Every time.

He tries to hold her.

DONNA: Teddy, you've already been doin too much for us. I can't pay ya back. It would be wrong to move in with ya right now.

TEDDY: It doesn't have to mean we haveta be man an wife right away. It's just...it could be just for a while. I want to help you get back on your feet. I mean, if only for Matthew's sake.

DONNA: I know...I know. But it's too soon.

A game whistle.

TEDDY: Why is everything always "too soon," Donna? Are we talkin about "him" now? Are we talkin about your ex again? Is it somethin I'm doin to ya? Somethin I did?

DONNA: I don't know.

TEDDY: Then what are we talkin about anyway? Would ya at least let me know what exactly the problem is between us? What I can do....

DONNA: We're too much trouble for ya. Already. I knew we would be.

TEDDY: I never back down from trouble. I want to be a father to Matthew. I want...to be a husband to you. There it is.

silence

DONNA: But you don't even know anythin about us.

TEDDY: I know I want to give your boy a good Christmas. I would like to.

Teddy has struck at one of Donna's fears.

DONNA: Don't ya think I been thinkin about that?

TEDDY: Troy an Matthew. They're gettin along great. They're buddies now. They're trainin partners. Why can't we be partners?

DONNA: Yeah. Now, it seems like they are. Gettin along.

TEDDY: Matthew likes me. You let me spend all that time with him.

DONNA: He needs to have some kinda father figure again. Someone to look up to. I know I'm not enough for him.

TEDDY: We could all have a family again.

pause

DONNA: But what kinda family, Teddy?

TEDDY: What do ya mean by that?

DONNA: You mean the..."family skate" kinda family. Everyone skatin to waltz music, holdin hands?

TEDDY: Well. Yeah. We could do that if ya want. *(laughs)* If we could ever get ya out there on the ice, we could do that.

pause

DONNA: Well, I don't believe in that kinda family any more. Maybe for some people, but not for me.

TEDDY: Why not?

silence

DONNA: Do ya remember how I...I lied an told ya I couldn't go skatin cause I broke my leg when I was little? Fallin down some stairs.

TEDDY: Now she comes outta left field with a hockey stick. What does this have to do with...?

DONNA: Well, I wasn't really so little when it happened. Kids ya can forgive if they have an accident

like that. Most people can anyway.

TEDDY: Huh?

DONNA: I didn't fall down those stairs. I was kinda...thrown...down them.

pause

TEDDY: Ya were.

DONNA: Yeah. *(tries to laugh)* **I was really...airborne.** *(laughs)* **Mom defies gravity.**

silence

TEDDY: What happened to you?

DONNA: Don't worry about me. I deserved all of mine.

TEDDY: How could someone deserve somethin like that?

She looks away. Her voice is quiet with rage and regret.

DONNA: Cause. I...let it all happen to Matthew, too. He didn't deserve anya his.

pause

TEDDY: How could ya stay with him...for eight years? If he was like that?

DONNA: Something changed when the baby came. *(laughs)* **Poor kid...turning out too much like me, not**

enough like him, I think. Eight years. *(pause)* **You might say I was a real...diehard.**

Teddy reaches for her. She doesn't move.

TEDDY: C'mere.

DONNA: So, now ya know...what you're gettin into. Invitin the likes of us to sleep over. Cause we're nothin but trouble. We can't seem to do anythin very fast. Like skate. Like...leave....

That does it. Donna is about to cry, but she fights it.

She doesn't let herself make a sound, and she wins.

TEDDY: Where is he? Where is this guy?

DONNA: Who cares.

TEDDY: I just want to wreck him, that's all. Cause, he's the real problem, isn't he? He's the one causin all the problems for us now!

DONNA: Teddy....

TEDDY: Cause everything would be fine, I know. If he weren't right there in the middle of us...!

DONNA: What did ya say?

Teddy stops short.

TEDDY: I just said, that's why I'd like to hurt him back. For what he did to you...an Matthew.

DONNA: I...I....

TEDDY: What? Donna. Sit down. Please. Keep talkin to me. Don't leave, okay? I...love you.

silence

DONNA: If I stay...can we just watch the game? An not talk anymore?

TEDDY: I'm not him. Sweetheart, how can I show ya I'm not him? I want to help ya forget about him.

DONNA: Believe me, Teddy. I want to.

TEDDY: This is probly the last, best chance I'm ever gonna have. I'm not gonna give up easy. I know it's not so easy to find someone. It's so damn close for us. It's killin me.

Teddy tries to focus on the game. For a few moments, they sit in silence, holding hands. Watching the children play.

DONNA: *(suddenly, to the players)* Get them, you guys. Go get them.

pause

TEDDY: Huh?

DONNA: *(shouts)* C'mon Leafs. Get em for us. C'mon Leafs! You're not makin anythin happen out there!

Donna rises.

TEDDY: Let's go fellas. Heads up! Let's get somethin goin, eh...?

DONNA: *(shouts)* Dry-clean the bums!... Dry-clean em! Dry clean their little arses!

TEDDY: What's into you now, anyways?

Donna builds herself into a frenzy.

DONNA: C'mon Leafs. You can do it. C'mon. Go Leafs. Leafs Leafs Leafs Leafs! Slaughter em...! Don't take no crap from them!

TEDDY: Jesus, look at her go, now....

DONNA: Go get em. Kick their butts! Knock em down! Give them...elbowmacaroni sandwiches!

TEDDY: Break outta the zone now! Let's go. Pass the puck. Look for the wingers!

DONNA: That's the way! KICK THEIR LILY-WHITE... SKATES OFF. CHECK THEM HARD! SKATE...!

TEDDY: Hey, we got a three on two. We got a three on two...!

Teddy moves forward.

Drop back, Troy! Drop pass, Adam! Drop pass...!

DONNA: Drop pass. C'mon guys! Let's go!

TEDDY: Adam!... What a HEADFAKE! Lost his UNDIES....

DONNA: He's right in front!

TEDDY: ...DEKE HIM!... DO ANOTHER HEAD-FAKE!...

DONNA: C'MON ADAM! MAKE THEM PAY!

TEDDY: YA GOT HIM. DEKE!... LIFT IT...UP!.. AH... AH.... Where...?

DONNA: The goalie got it. It's under him.

Teddy crumbles. A whistle blows.

TEDDY: That stupid...stupid...stupid! Blew it. Of all the stupid plays, stupid friggin shots....

DONNA: *(excited)* **It was so close, though. You were right about them hearin us. We helped make that happen, didn't we?**

He leans over the boards.

TEDDY: *(shouts)* **That's when ya should shoot, ya stupid idiot. When he lays down on the damn goal line!**

DONNA: *(shouts)* **Yeah, Adam! Shoot it next time! We need a score!**

TEDDY: *(louder)* **Hey, ya little Tomahawk! If you'd make a few morea those insteada blowin them, we might get outta the basement someday.**

Game play resumes.

silence

DONNA: That was kinda cruel, wasn't it?

TEDDY: Hey. I'm just tryin to get under his skin with it. Ya gotta get under their skins if we want to have any effect on them.

Donna is uncertain, guilty about her role in it.

DONNA: I think I'm gonna go wait in the car.

TEDDY: Why? Things are pickin up now.

DONNA: Nothin. I kinda got a lot to think about.

TEDDY: We made a real break today, didn't we? Talkin about things.

DONNA: Yeah. We did.

TEDDY: We got a lot more things...I'm kinda back into the game now. Maybe we got a chance here. Hey...what's?...

She is about to leave. There is the sound of cheering.

SCORES!... We scored! *(shouts)* **Way to go, boys! Way to come back.... No Shutout! NOOOOOOO SHUTOUT! We broke the shutout!**

DONNA: Who was it?

TEDDY: Adam. It was Adam! See what I told ya? We got under his skin, then he went an scored for us. On the next play. See? He didn't go screw it up this time. We motivated him. We oughta get an assist! Way to go, Adam buddy! That's the way to burn their wagons! Good heads up! That's the way to...!

DONNA: Take it easy, Teddy....

Something out on the ice stops Teddy short.

TEDDY: *(to Donna)* **Did you see that? Did you see what that little brat just did? He gave me the finger.**

DONNA: Actually, he kinda gave ya the whole glove.

TEDDY: *(yells)* **Hey Adam! Can't ya see I'm on your side here?**

Game play resumes

DONNA: I'll see ya after, okay? I'll see ya....

TEDDY: Donna...wait a second...!

Donna lingers on the top step of the bleachers.

Teddy is torn between following her, and watching the game.

He is mesmerized by the action on the ice, and stays.

Scene 7

The next weekend. Near the end of a game. The sound of the game is heard rising in the dark. A whistle blast. Teddy enters, frustrated.

DONNA: What did the coach say?

TEDDY: Nothin intelligent. He doesn't even got the brains God gave a flea....

DONNA: He's not gonna put him out?

TEDDY: He's only gonna doubleshift Troy for the last minutea the game insteada the whole three. How's he ever gonna make any kinda impression on the rep coach in only a minute?

A buzzer sounds. Game play resumes.

DONNA: I don't think we can come back anyway. They're too fast for us.

TEDDY: They're not fast. They're just dirty. They're goons. They're a buncha pint-sized goons. They only look fast cause our team are lyin horizontal all the time....

DONNA: They do make a lot of dirty plays.

TEDDY: They're knockin us down everywhere. Dirty hits! All dirty hits. Can't that coach see the importance of havin Troy out there in a game like this? He's the enforcer. He's gotta protect our little guys.

DONNA: Well. The game's almost over, anyway. We'll have to get them another day.

TEDDY: That's great. Except the rep coach isn't gonna be here another time. An we're not gonna get him to come here another time, cause we're last place. He's here to scout the Whalers, he ain't here to see us.

pause

DONNA: Teddy. It's not the end of the world. Troy's gonna have other chances. Next week, next year. Relax.

TEDDY: There's no next year. Next year starts *today.* Troy hasn't done nothin today! I tell him, if he works hard, he can make his mark, things'll happen for him....

DONNA: Well, that's a good thing to say....

TEDDY: But he's not makin any mark. He's like a big pylon out there. The game's goin by...my son...nothin's gonna happen for him...no flash....

DONNA: Teddy. Relax. You know it's only a game.

TEDDY: I know it's only a game. But it's the only game. I been workin so hard with him. I'm so sick an tired to death of losin. Every single time out.... *(agitated again)* These dirty Whalers. They did it to us again. We didn't learn anythin....

DONNA: Hey. I got a great idea. Afterwards, we can go down to Kate's. All four of us. Get a treat for the kids. Maybe go to the video store. *(winks)* We won't go to the horror section, but I bet we could find....

Game play resumes. Teddy sits up.

TEDDY: Troy? Troy's out! Look! The coach put him out with a minute anten to go. He's bein double-shifted! *(shouts)* My boy is bein double-shifted!...

He is ecstatic. He rushes down to the boards.

DONNA: Let's go Troy. Go Leafs! Let's get a goal! Never say die.

TEDDY: Dig in there Dunner! Look for your left winger! Look up the left side!

DONNA: Take it out, guys. Watch your offsides!

TEDDY: Troy! LEFT WING, TROY! LEFT WING! You're a left winger!

DONNA: You can do it, Troy!

TEDDY: *(yells)* Troy! If ya get the puck, just friggin go with it. Just go with it. Don't bother passin it to anyone!

DONNA: Go get it, Ryan! It's all yours, Ryan! C'mon.

TEDDY: Ryan! Don't give it away like that with a minute ta go! Ya can't score from the goddamn red line!

DONNA: Chase them back!

Teddy anxiously watches the clock.

TEDDY: Forty seconds. He can't do nothin in forty seconds. This is pointless.

DONNA: Stay on him, Troy! Force him back.

TEDDY: Forecheck, Troy! Forecheck! That's your man! Pester him.

DONNA: Stay on him, Troy! Don't give up.

TEDDY: Wear him out. Pokecheck.

DONNA: C'mon...!

TEDDY: Time's runnin out, Troy! Pokecheck! Forecheck! Do anythin...!

Suddenly....

DONNA: He's got it. In front...! Go...!

TEDDY: *(shrieking)* **GO TO THE NET, TROY! GO TO THE NET! DON'T PASS IT!...SLAP....**

DONNA: Skate! Troy! There's someone behind ya!...

TEDDY: MAN-ON, TROY! MAN ON! DON'T WAIT! SLAP IT!

DONNA: TROY...!

TEDDY: SHOOT...!

Teddy screams. He goes white.

DONNA: Oh my God.... Did you see that?

TEDDY: *(choked)* **Ref...? Ref!...**

DONNA: He was all alone in front.

The game continues.Teddy finds his voice.

TEDDY: *(shrieks)* **PENALTY SHOT! THAT...IS A PENALTY SHOT, YOU IDIOT! DO YOU KNOW...THE FRIGGIN RULESA THIS GAME? STOP TH...STOP....**

DONNA: It's all over. There's only ten seconds left.

TEDDY: DO YOU KNOW WHEN TO CALL A PENALTY SHOT? DO YOU KNOW WHAT HAPPENS IN HOCKEY WHEN SOMEONE GETS ASSAULTED WHEN THEY'RE ALL ALONE IN FRONT OF THE NET?...

THERE IS A COACH FROM THE REP TEAM SITTIN OVER THERE! WHY DON'T YA ASK HIM?!

A sound of cheering begins.

DONNA: *(shouts)* **Ya should call some penalties, Referee. That wasn't fair at all...!**

TEDDY: *(hoarse)* **We owe you little buggers. From last time. We still owe you. We....**

A buzzer sounds.

The cheering reaches full volume, then gradually dies.

DONNA: If only Troy coulda gone a little faster. He'd have scored easy, I bet.

TEDDY: He shoulda shot. He...when he had the chance. He had the chance....

DONNA: He had a nice try. He stole the puck from the defence, all by himself....

TEDDY: I know. He...he's no quitter, Troy.

DONNA: It was such a good play, too. He did what ya yelled to him an he got the puck.

TEDDY: He coulda scored, though. On a penalty shot. The drama of it. It woulda been incredible....

DONNA: I bet he scores next time. Live and learn.

Donna puts her arm around him. Teddy is shaky, hiding his face. He looks like he might cry.

TEDDY: Don't shake hands with him, Troy. Don't shake hands with that little creep.

DONNA: What?

Teddy moves down toward the boards again.

TEDDY: Don't shake hands with him, Troy! Don't you dare shake hands with him! After what he did to you? Don't you dare shake hands with anya them!

DONNA: Teddy. The game's over...!

She tries to lead him by the arm. He never takes his eyes off the ice.

TEDDY: Don't shake his hand, Troy! Don't you dare shake that hand! Get him back for that! He's laughin at us. NOW! Give him one! Give him one back!

Donna drops his arm. Teddy is vicious. She takes a backward step up the bleachers.

DONNA: Teddy...? *(choked)* **Don't....**

TEDDY: YES! YES! That's it.... DID THAT GET YOUR ATTENTION, YA LITTLE PIECEA....! Give it to him Troy! Give it.... *(pause)* **Get his helmet off! Ya can't get his jersey over his helmet! YEAH. WAIL ON HIM! JUST WAIL ON HIM! DON'T LET HIM BREATHE!**

Donna is frozen. She can't move, doesn't want to believe what she is seeing.

YEAH...EVERYBODY UP! LET'S DANCE! EVERY-BODY. GRAB SOMEONE! PAY THEM BACK FOR LAST TIME...! SHOW THEM WHO THE REAL LOSERS

ARE! LET'S GO...MATTHEW...!

It has become a brawl. The crowd is cheering.

DONNA: M...Matthew...?

TEDDY: C'MON MATTHEW! DON'T TAKE ANYTHIN OFF THAT KID! Do him up like I showed ya. C'MON, BUDDY...YOU CAN DO IT!

DONNA: Matthew? MATTHEW!

There is the sound of children crying. Donna searches frantically through the bodies for her son.

TEDDY: OH!... Look at MR. REF! NOW, he's gonna call some PENALTIES! *(sings)* **THREE BLIND REFS! BLIND, BLIND, BLIND!**

DONNA: MATTHEW! GET OFF HIM...! GET AWAY FROM HIM...!

TEDDY: Hey, leave him alone. He's winnin! He's on top. He's got him licked...!

DONNA: MATTHEW? MATTHEW! GO! GET OVER THE BENCH. GET AWAY FROM THEM!

Donna tries to climb over the boards but Teddy stops her.

TEDDY: *(laughs)* **Hey. Where the hell do ya think you're goin? He's okay.**

DONNA: Look...what ya did. Look....

TEDDY: Ya can't go out there. There's a fight goin

on. Haven't ya noticed? Matthew's did fine! He did fine for himself. He *won*....

Donna stops struggling, fixes on Teddy.

DONNA: He won.

TEDDY: What? It was just a little scrap. Calm down. We won it. Our team won the fight.

DONNA: Our kids.... Look...what ya *started*...!

pause

TEDDY: Whaddya mean? I didn't start it. *They* started it. The ref started it by bein blind.

DONNA: Ya told Troy to punch that player. When they were gonna just shake hands...!

TEDDY: Donna. It was a fight. They happen sometimes. We had ta send them a message, y'know? We had to fight back. Hey, it wasn't even a real scrap either. The whole thing was over in about half a minute. They barely even got their gloves off, their... masks off....

silence

DONNA: How could ya do somethin like this? How could ya?

TEDDY: I'm sorry it had to happen like that, but hey....

DONNA: Don't touch me. Take your hand off me.

He tries to hold her.

TEDDY: Donna, you're takin this a little too....

DONNA: GET AWAY FROM US! I DON'T WANT YA...! NEAR US!

silence

TEDDY: Okay. If I got a little carried away...in the heat of the moment....

DONNA: *(spits)* "Carried away," ya got.

TEDDY: I was just fired up. It wasn't fair to our boys!

DONNA: Ya got a little carried away, Teddy! When ya...ya taught my son how ta fight...how to hit people. Ya showed him. Then...ya put him in a fight. Ya....

TEDDY: We worked on some boxin. We worked on a lotta things. For conditioning....

DONNA: So...So.... Ya practised...how to hurt people? How to beat someone up. Ya told him...it's okay...it's normal.... It's normal.... It's fun...ya practised. *(pause)* All the time I been tryin to teach him... it's not okay...it's not normal...it's....

TEDDY: I told ya. I was teachin him to take care of himself.

DONNA: Ya put my baby in a fight! After I went out an told ya what happened to him before, Teddy? Are ya stupid? Or are ya just heartless?

silence

TEDDY: Well, I...I...figured...he'd be able to fight

back...not haveta be scared any more. It'd give him... a little confidence...since...what ya told me.

DONNA: Confidence...to do what? To what? To grab someone and whale on them! Is that what...ya want him to have...the confidence to do...? You made my boy fight...cause you wanted to send a message to a bunch of eight-year-olds!

silence

TEDDY: Okay. I...maybe...shouldn'ta done that. Tell Troy to throw that first punch....

DONNA: God. I was gonna move in with you. I was gonna do it all again.

pause

TEDDY: You were? Gonna move in with me? What do ya mean...ya were?

DONNA: *(more to self)* **I saw it coming. Only I didn't want to look.**

Donna gathers up her things to leave.

TEDDY: If ya want me to say I'm sorry. Then, I'm sorry. I shoulda been more sensitive. There. Okay?

He stops her.

DONNA: Don't. I really need to go now.

TEDDY: Hey, I don't think you understand some things here.

DONNA: I think I understand plenty.

TEDDY: No! Cause if you did, you'd know that I tried to give something to your boy that would make him feel safe for once. Jeez, you're his mom. You'd think you'd want him to be prepared for somethin like this. When it happens. And it does happen, Donna! Ya can't stick your head in the sand and think the whole friggin world is like Sesame Street. Hey, I'd like it, too. I bet no one writes rude graffiti on the walls of Sesame Street. But what happened on the ice here? It wasn't pretty, sure, but it was real, and your Matthew was ready for it.

pause

DONNA: Yeah. He was more than ready.

TEDDY: Sure. Ya want him to grow up defenseless? Is that it? Ya can't want that. He *has* to know how to protect himself. Cause he's not...by nature...he's not strong....

DONNA: I know. He's got no protections by nature. *(pause)* Not even me.

She pushes past him. He gets in her way.

TEDDY: What? What are ya tellin me here, Donna?

DONNA: I have to go get my son. Excuse me.

TEDDY: Are ya sayin I blew it? Over this...?

DONNA: We're nothin to you, Teddy.

TEDDY: Okay. Okay. Okay. Let's just talk for a second. I...I just got carried away over a game. It doesn't mean we have to...break up. It doesn't mean that. We

need each other. I was in the heat of the moment. It doesn't mean ya have to give up on us. Please. We both need this....

She speaks over him, stopping him short.

DONNA: My son is sittin over there in the penalty box, starin at us. He's watchin us cause we're his only protection. He's wearin a buncha pads from a flea market. Onea the first things you ever said to me was...don't worry, its rough but Matthew's got...protection. *(pause)* **But Matthew, he's really got no protection at all. Cause I'm a pushover. Y'know? An I'm desperate, too. I needed this more than you'll ever know. But I don't need to trust my only baby boy to the heat of the moment. Cause I know, now. I know the...the "heat of the moment" and "carried away" are just really bad excuses for makin someone bleed if ya want them to.** *(pause)* **There's just too many moments in a whole life, Teddy. But there's only onea him.**

pause

TEDDY: It was just...a stupid game. That's all it was.

pause

DONNA: You take carea yourself, okay? We have to go now.

TEDDY: So. I blew it. Didn't I? I really...blew it. *(pause)* **Same as always.**

Teddy is very still.

He exits.

silence

Donna looks out over the ice.

DONNA: Matthew? Come on outta there. W...we have to go home now. Okay? Your penalty's over, sweetheart. Everyone's gone home now. There'll be people comin in. They're gonna start skatin. An the big tractor's comin out soon. *(pause)* **So, you're gonna stay in the penalty box overnight, huh? That's a long penalty, isn't it?**

The sound of the zamboni, warming up.

Matthew. Ya don't want to stay overnight in here. There's probly bats in the rink. An you don't like bats. Mommy doesn't like em, that's for sure. Alright. I'm coming to get you.

She opens the gate, and steps onto the ice.

Matthew?

Donna realizes where she is. She grabs onto the boards, and holds on for dear life.

Matthew! Look where Mom is. Look...Mom's out on the ice. See? So...ya...better...come help her? She might just kill herself out here.

Music for the family skate rises, as Donna edges along the boards.

The lights dim, but not *to black.*

Scene 8

It is six weeks later. Before a game. Donna is sitting in the bleachers, alone. She is sipping coffee. Teddy enters quietly, behind her. He is carrying a rose.

He watches her, then decides to hide the flower underneath his jacket, but doesn't anticipate the thorns. Donna turns and notices him.

TEDDY: Ow. Hey....

silence

DONNA: Hi.

pause

TEDDY: Long time no see, eh? You're.... You're here bright an early, aren't ya?

pause

DONNA: That's me. The early worm. Figured I'd get my usual good seat.

Teddy stands, awkwardly.

TEDDY: So. How was your Christmas?

DONNA: Well, the Grinch stole it. Other than that, it wasn't too bad.

TEDDY: *(laughs)* **Oh yeah? The Grinch stole it. That's very funny.**

DONNA: Yeah. Not if you're a Who.

TEDDY: A...what? Who?

DONNA: A Who.

TEDDY: *(looking behind him)* Where?

DONNA: Forget it.

Donna looks around. She pretends to read something on the scoreboard. Teddy wants to move closer.

TEDDY: Yeah. Ya know...Troy...got a suspension. He got a six weeks suspension. This is his first game back today. Playin the Jets today.

DONNA: How is he? How's Troy doin?

pause

TEDDY: Uh, the ex—his mom—was wonderin if Troy...an Matthew...could still, uh, play together after school some days. *(pause)* I...I won't be around. It'd be over at her house downtown, so you wouldn't have to worry that I'd be there. Cause, I wouldn't. *(pause)* So, if it's okay with you, just have Matthew give...Troy a call. You still got the number, don't ya?

DONNA: I think that might be alright. If Matthew wants.

TEDDY: Sure. Alright. Well. That's the only reason I came over. I'm gonna go sit back over there, now. I'll see ya around, eh?

He starts to exit, then stops. He painfully withdraws the rose from underneath his jacket.

He thrusts it at her.

DONNA: What am I supposed to do with that?

TEDDY: Uh...I don't know. Put it in a vase? Or somethin.

She smiles, but doesn't take it.

DONNA: Thanks.

TEDDY: Hey. You can always compost it.

He lays it beside her, moves to exit.

DONNA: Hey.

TEDDY: Yeah?

He stops.

DONNA: You okay. Teddy?

TEDDY: Me? Yeah. Fine. I'm alright. Fine. Yeah. Sure.

DONNA: That's good. Me too.

TEDDY: So how, how's Matthew? How's he doin?

DONNA: He lost a tooth. He lost his first tooth last week.

TEDDY: Did he? Well, that's just great.

DONNA: **He's been waitin for the tooth fairy. She's still rolling pennies.**

TEDDY: *(laughs)* **Well, you tell him, Teddy said, the tooth fairy loves hockey players.**

DONNA: *(laughs along)* **Yeah. But I bet she's not married to one.**

The laughter stops, as a buzzer sounds.

TEDDY: **Guess it's about to start, huh?**

pause

DONNA: **If ya want to stay here an watch the game. That'd be...okay.**

TEDDY: **Na, I wouldn't want to make ya uncomfortable.**

DONNA: **It's alright. I wouldn't mind the company. Even yours.**

She clears a place for him.

TEDDY: **Thanks, Donna. I been really kinda itchin to get back in here.**

DONNA: **Just don't go shoutin in my ear, alright? I'm just startin to get my hearin back.**

TEDDY: **Okay. I won't. I won't....**

The game begins. Teddy and Donna lean forward.

When the puck is dropped the lights begin to fade slowly, as the action rises.

DONNA: *(shouts)* **Okay, team. Skate hard out there. Go get em.**

TEDDY: Let's go Leafs. Gonna shoot down these Jets.

DONNA: Alright. Headsup now! Stay sharp!

TEDDY: Sticks on the ice. Let's play good hockey!

DONNA: They don't got a chance do they guys? Skate hard!

TEDDY: Yeah. It's all over for em, isn't it?

DONNA: Yeah. They don't got a chance...!

TEDDY: It's all over. Right...?

DONNA: It's all over....

Donna and Teddy's voices trail off, as they look at each other, for a searching moment.

Just as the light disappears.

The sound of the game rises in the dark.

END

About Michael Melski

AN AWARD-WINNING WRITER AND FILMMAKER from Cape Breton, Nova Scotia, Michael Melski's many plays, including the previously published *Joyride* and *Caribou*, have been produced across Canada. He was playwright in residence at The Shaw Festival, as well as a screenwriting resident at Norman Jewison's Canadian Film Centre. His film work includes "Mile Zero," "Touch and Go," and "Serenade." For television, he wrote for the acclaimed drama "Straight Up" and is currently writing on the crime series "Blue Murder." His first book of two plays, *Blood on Steel*, was published in 1996 by University College of Cape Breton Press, and he was hailed as "an important new voice in Canadian fiction."

Before he entered the show business arena, Michael captained his own Peewee Leafs to the Cape Breton County Minor Hockey Championship for two consecutive seasons (1979-80). Despite his age and physical condition, he still hopes to one day play in the NHL.

Hockey Mom, Hockey Dad was first produced by Brou-ha-ha Theatre at Café Olé in Halifax on February 8, 1995. The production was directed by Jean Morpurgo with stage management by Gillian

Mahen. TEDDY: Steven Manuel. DONNA: Irene Poole. The Touring Production of *Hockey Mom, Hockey Dad* was produced by Two Planks and a Passion Theatre. The production opened October 4, 2000, and was directed by Ken Schwartz with stage management by Donna MacMillan. Set design by Ian Pygott and original music score by Jeff Hennessy. TEDDY: Gordon Gammie. DONNA: Chris O'Neill and Jackie Torrens.

Notes from Michael Melski

THIS IS A PLAY FOR MY FRIENDS, THEN. We were a dirty bunch, fully deserving of the litter that was thrown at us by the rink rat girls we teased. No Guy Lafleur's goldilocks or Sittler's Wheatabix for us. We were the Broad Street Bullies, Caper style. Ten and under, pretend-Flyers spat from exhaust pipes splayed arse over tit across ice in Coachie's fierce diagrams. Bobby Clarke, our idol, his gap-toothed fearless diabetic brilliance on the ice made our lives sweeter. We picked fights for the fans, the moms and dads, swore a blue-line streak, dead last, and the shit really hit the fan when we got home.

This is also a play for my Uncle Ches. He was a kid from the Pier who made it to the Montreal Junior Canadiens, once faced Jacques Plante on a breakaway and missed, later crashed into a goal post in full flight, ruptured a kidney, then took eight years to die on dialysis. But he almost made it.

This is a play for my friends, now. Some of them married some of the girls that used to throw garbage at us. Some of them are raising their own little Bobby (and Bobbie) Clarkes now. For whole families of rink rats, busted hearts, intact, playing the great game, same as same....

Assists

AS GOOD AS A GOAL in making this play and publication a reality, the author would like to thank Bernard and Mary Melski, Coach Bob Callie, Steven Manuel, Irene Poole, Jean Morpurgo, Scott Banks, Gillian Mahen, Ken Schwartz and Chris O'Neill, Marianne Ward, Kellie Marie Redcliffe, Jeff Hennessy, Ian Pygott, Donna MacMillan, Gordon Gammie, Jackie Torrens, Condon MacLeod, Theatre 21st Century, The Shaw Festival, Al Magee, The Canada Council, Wendy MacKeigan, the Harold Greenberg Fund, the Nova Scotia Arts Council, and especially Ron Caplan and Bonnie Thompson at Breton Books.

ALSO AVAILABLE FROM
Breton Books

As True As I'm Sittin' Here

200 CAPE BRETON STORIES

collected by Archie Neil Chisholm

edited by Brian Sutcliffe and Ronald Caplan

LAUGHS, COMEBACKS, ghosts, fairies, put-downs, and all-round wit—from Dan Angus Beaton, Jim St. Clair, Sid Timmons, Hector Doink MacDonald, Annie the Tailor MacPhee, Archie Neil Chisholm, Alex John MacIsaac, Paddy MacDonald, and many more. Stories that shorten the road, lighten the work, and fill the pauses between tunes, from settings where good stories are born and thrive—kitchens and living rooms throughout Cape Breton Island.

34 STORYTELLERS • 220 PAGES • $22.50

Early Cape Breton

FROM FOUNDING TO FAMINE

by Robert Morgan

A COLLECTION OF ESSAYS, TALKS, AND CONVERSATIONS, from a warm, deeply-informed scholar who has kept history alive *and* accurate.

We see the Founding of the independent Cape Breton Colony, its extraordinary first Lieutenant-Governor J.F.W. DesBarres, and the coming of the Loyalists; the internal squabbles that held back development and resulted in the 1820 annexation of Cape Breton to mainland Nova Scotia, the struggle for Separation—and the upheaval of the Great Famine that restructured the fabric of Cape Breton.

PHOTOS • 176 PAGES • $21.50

In the Pit

A CAPE BRETON COAL MINER

by Rennie MacKenzie

A RARE, EXCITING insider's story of coal mine life. There are no strikes or explosions here—just the gripping drama and rich good humour of one man's daily work underground, from the brute shoveling at the coal face and hand-shifting tons of shaker pans, to hurling through low, narrow tunnels testing a diesel during early mechanization. You are not spared the details.

Rennie MacKenzie worked 18 years in Number 12 Colliery, New Waterford. Then he left the mines, went to college, and served as a United Church minister for 35 years. He has retired to New Waterford, where he lives with his wife Norma. Their love affair and family trials are a powerful thread through his remarkable book.

PHOTOS • 176 PAGES • $21.50

• PRICES INCLUDE GST & POSTAGE IN CANADA •

CONTINUED ON NEXT PAGE

ALSO AVAILABLE FROM

Breton Books

www.capebretonbooks.com

Cape Breton Shipwreck Stories

1761-1955

collected & edited by Ronald Caplan

FROM THE GUT-WRENCHING TREK of the *Auguste*'s survivors to John Angus Fraser's hilarious adventures aboard the *Kismet II*, to Walter Boudreau's harrowing account of days adrift in a lifeboat while his companions died around him—a batch of good stories from Cape Breton shipwrecks, told by survivors, rescuers and passionate researchers.

From eyewitness accounts to kitchen memories, from fiction to song—these are lasting, enjoyable and often painful stories.

PHOTOS • 176 PAGES • $18.50

Cape Breton Works

MORE LIVES FROM CAPE BRETON'S MAGAZINE

edited by Ronald Caplan

THIS IS CAPE BRETON TALKING! This extraordinary mix of men's and women's lives delivers a solid dose of the courage, humour and good storytelling that make a place like Cape Breton work.

From Canada's longest-running oral history journal, these voices affirm, entertain, and inspire—and carry our stories to the world.

154 PHOTOS • 300 PAGES • $23.50

The Highland Heart in Nova Scotia

by Neil MacNeil

NEW EDITION CELEBRATES 50 YEARS of a remarkable Cape Breton Classic!

The Highland Heart in Nova Scotia is Neil MacNeil's memoir of his boyhood. This is Cape Breton pioneer history writ large, with all the purity and bravado and passion that an exiled native son brings to the world of his heart and his youth.

Wonderful writing about the peace and raw humour of Celtic Cape Breton's Golden Age, with ample doses of history and of legend.

PHOTOS • 208 PAGES • $18.50

• PRICES INCLUDE GST & POSTAGE IN CANADA •

ALSO AVAILABLE FROM

Breton Books

www.capebretonbooks.com

Father Jimmy

LIFE AND TIMES OF JIMMY TOMPKINS

by Jim Lotz and Michael R. Welton

THE ABRASIVE, COMPASSIONATE, nagging, cranky, inquisitive, generous, altogether marvelous priest from Margaree—spiritual father of the co-op movement in Nova Scotia; still its inspiration and conscience. Angered by injustice, fortified by compassion and faith, Tompkins encouraged cooperation, self-reliance and adult education to get people to make a difference in their own lives.

The roots of the worldwide Antigonish Movement—an enjoyable biography, and a tool for today.

PHOTOS • 176 PAGES • $18.50

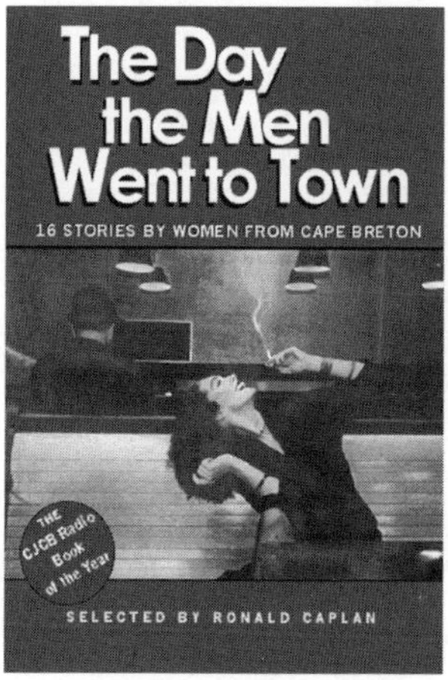

The Day the Men Went to Town

16 STORIES BY WOMEN FROM CAPE BRETON

STRONG WRITING by women who have a significant attachment to Cape Breton Island! These stories are about fisherwomen and aliens from space, the poignancy of family life and tragedy in the coal mines—and several approaches to love. Entertaining and thought-provoking.

By Lynn Coady, Joan Clark, Claudia Gahlinger, Beatrice MacNeil, Susan Zettell, Sherry D. Ramsey, Jean McNeil, Kim Williamson, Tessie Gillis, Ann-Marie MacDonald, D.C. Troicuk, Tricia Fish, Erin McNamara, Teresa O'Brien, Ellen Frith, Carol Bruneau.

176 PAGES • $18.50

The Irish in Cape Breton

by A. A. MacKenzie

A RARE, RICH AND LIVELY history of the Irish in Cape Breton, once again showing that the recipe for authentic Cape Breton is a complex and exciting mix. MacKenzie offers here an excellent general introduction to the Irish experience and their contribution, a book stocked with details about both culture and individuals.

With an essay on Cape Breton's Irish Music by Paul M. MacDonald, and the cover painting by Bob Fitzgerald of "White Point, circa 1935."

160 PAGES • $18.50

• PRICES INCLUDE GST & POSTAGE IN CANADA •

CONTINUED ON NEXT PAGE